☀ ☀ ☀ ☀ ☀ ☀ ☀ ☀ ☀ ☀ ☀ ☀ ☀ ☀ ☀

HOPEFUL AS THE BREAK OF DAY.

THOMAS BAILEY ALDRICH (1836–1907)

I'm filled with joy
when the day dawns quietly
over the roof of the sky.

FROM AN ESKIMO SONG

Each day the first day:
Each day a life.

DAG HAMMARSKJÖLD (1905–1961)

I live a day at a time.
Each day I look for a kernel
of excitement. In the morning,
I say: "What is my exciting thing
for today?" Then, I do the day.
Don't ask me about tomorrow.

BARBARA JORDAN

A HELEN EXLEY GIFTBOOK

hope!
dream!

PICTURES BY JOANNA KIDNEY

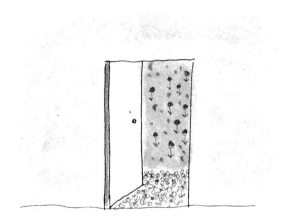

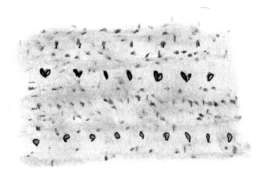

The first sparrow of Spring!
The year beginning
    with younger hope than ever!

HENRY DAVID THOREAU (1817–1862)

The old happiness is withered
        and dead.
But, see, there is a greenness
        veiling the land...
    the frail beginnings
            of a new and better life.

PAM BROWN, B.1928

[There] is a need
to find
and sing our own song,
to stretch our limbs
and shake them in a dance
so wild
that nothing can roost there,
that stirs the yearning
for solitary voyage.

BARBARA LAZEAR ASCHER,
FROM "PLAYING AFTER DARK"

I think that wherever
your journey takes you,
there are new gods waiting there,
with divine patience –
and laughter.

SUSAN M. WATKINS, B.1945

Go confidently in the direction
of your dreams!
Live the life you've imagined.

HENRY DAVID THOREAU (1817–1862)

*Our little boats set sail
on an unknown ocean –
and at this we are afraid.
But we are a part of wonder.
The sea is bright with marvels,
the sky is awash with stars.
And we are alive
in the midst of them.*

PAM BROWN, B.1928

When the sun is shining
I can do anything;
    no mountain is too high,
no trouble too difficult
    to overcome.

WILMA RUDOLPH, B.1940

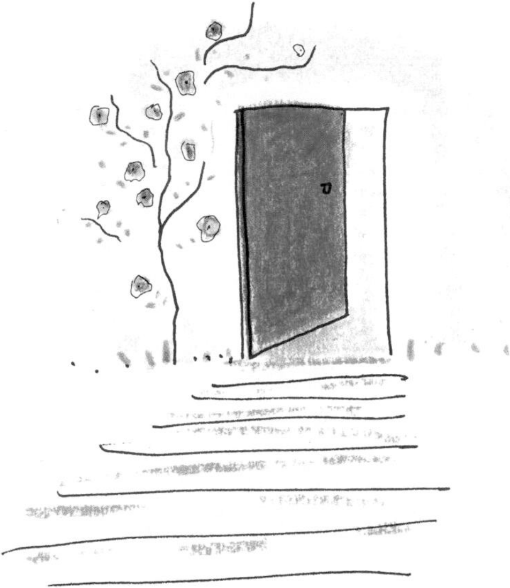

WAKE UP WITH A SMILE
AND GO AFTER LIFE…
LIVE IT,
ENJOY IT,
TASTE IT,
SMELL IT,
FEEL IT.

JOE KNAPP

Keep a green tree
in your heart
and perhaps the singing
bird will come.

CHINESE PROVERB

I want to see de children
wake up happy to de sunrise...
I want to see de loss of hope
everywhere replace wid de
win of living

GRACE NICHOLS, B.1950,
FROM "CARIBBEAN WOMAN PRAYER"

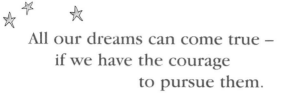

All our dreams can come true –
if we have the courage
   to pursue them.

WALT DISNEY (1901–1966)

*Don't be afraid of the space
between your dreams and reality.
If you can dream it,
you can make it so.*

BELVA DAVIS, B.1932

We are all in the gutter,
but
some of us
are looking
at the stars.

OSCAR WILDE (1854–1900),
FROM "LADY WINDERMERE'S FAN"

It seems to me
that we can never give up
longing and wishing,
while we are thoroughly alive.
There are certain things
we feel to be beautiful
and good,
and we must hunger after them.

GEORGE ELIOT
[MARY ANN EVANS]
(1819-1880)

Each second
there can be
a new beginning.
It is choice.
It is your choice.

CLEARWATER

*You can have anything
you want
    if you want it
      desperately enough.
You must want it
    with an exuberance
  that erupts through the skin
        and joins the energy
    that created the world.*

SHEILA GRAHAM

You have your brush,
   you have your colours,
you paint PARADISE,
   then in you go.

NIKOS KAZANTZAKIS (1885–1957)

Take time to dream –
It is hitching your wagon to a star.
Take time to love and to be loved –
It is the privilege of the gods.
Take time to look around –
It is too short a day to be closed in.
Take time to laugh –
It is the music of the soul.

OLD ENGLISH PRAYER

Every blade of grass,

each leaf,

each separate floret and petal,

is an inscription

speaking of hope.

RICHARD JEFFERIES (1848–1887)

Hope is the pillar
that holds up the world.

PLINY THE ELDER (23–79)

Hope is a microscopic seed
from which great things can grow –
courage and kindness, patience,
endurance, love.

CHARLOTTE GRAY, B.1937

Everything that is done in the world
is done by hope.

MARTIN LUTHER (1483–1546)

*I've dreamt in my life
dreams that have stayed with me
ever after,
and changed my ideas:
  they've gone through*

and through me,
      like wine through water,
and altered the colour
            of my mind.

EMILY BRONTË (1818–1848)

A ROCK PILE
CEASES TO BE A ROCK PILE
THE MOMENT
A SINGLE MAN CONTEMPLATES IT,
BEARING WITHIN HIM
THE IMAGE OF A CATHEDRAL.

ANTOINE DE SAINT-EXUPÉRY (1900–1944)

Hope sees the invisible,
feels the intangible and achieves
the impossible.

AUTHOR UNKNOWN

A new life begins for us

with every second.

Let us go forward joyously to meet it.

We must press on,

whether we will or no,

and we shall walk better

with our eyes before us

than with them ever cast behind.

JEROME K. JEROME (1859–1927)

 ADVENTURE!

There isn't a train
I wouldn't take,
   no matter where it's going.

EDNA ST. VINCENT MILLAY (1892–1950)

I hear a locomotive's whistle
   in the night, far-away places
shout their longing
and I turn over in my bed
   and think "Travelling!"

KURT TUCHOLSKY (1890–1935)

If I had my life to live over,

I would start barefoot earlier in the spring

and stay that way

later in the fall.

I would go to more dances.

I would ride more merry-go-rounds.

I would pick more daisies.

NADINE STAIR

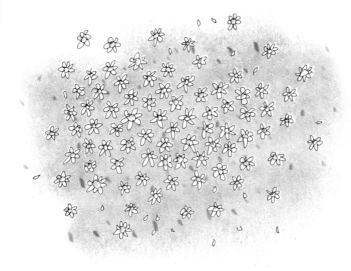

Hold fast your dreams!
Within your heart
keep one still, secret spot
where dreams may go
and, sheltered so,
may thrive and grow.

LOUISE DRISCOLL

*Inside myself is a place
where I live all alone and that's where
you renew your springs
that never dry up.*

PEARL BUCK (1892–1973)

Hope, like faith, is nothing
if it is not courageous;
it is nothing if it is not ridiculous.

THORNTON WILDER (1897–1976),
FROM "THE EIGHTH DAY"

"ON WITH THE DANCE,
LET JOY BE UNCONFINED"
IS MY MOTTO,
WHETHER THERE'S
ANY DANCE TO DANCE
OR ANY JOY TO UNCONFINE.

MARK TWAIN (1835–1910)

Far away there in the sunshine
are my highest aspirations –
I may not reach them, but I can look up
and see their beauty,
believe in them...

LOUISA MAY ALCOTT (1832–1888)

*Climb the mountains
and get their good tidings.
Nature's peace will flow
into you as sunshine flows into trees.*

JOHN MUIR (1838–1914)

HOPE, CHILD,
TOMORROW AND TOMORROW STILL,
AND EVERY TOMORROW HOPE;
TRUST WHILE YOU LIVE.

VICTOR HUGO (1802–1885)

You are everything that is,
your thoughts, your life,
your dreams come true.
You are everything you choose to be.
You are as unlimited
as the endless universe.

SHAD HELMSTETTER

I believe in the sun,
even when it is not shining.
I believe in love,
even when I do not feel it.

*

Believe in life!
Always human beings will live
and progress
to greater, broader, and fuller life.

W.E.B. DU BOIS (1868–1963)

ALL ACTS PERFORMED IN THE WORLD
BEGIN
IN THE IMAGINATION.

BARBARA GRIZZUTI HARRISON
(1941–2002)

If one is lucky,
a solitary fantasy can totally transform
one million realities.

MAYA ANGELOU, B.1928

From dreams
are made the precious
and imperishable things,
whose loveliness
lives on,
and does not fade.

VIRNA SHEARD

This fire in me...
– it's the hunger
of all my people back of me,
from all ages,
for light,
for the life higher!

ANZIA YEZIERSKA (C.1885–1970),
FROM "HUNGRY HEARTS"

Life is no "brief candle" to me.
It is a sort of splendid torch
which I have got hold of for a moment,
and I want
to make it burn as brightly
as possible
before handing it on
to future generations.

GEORGE BERNARD SHAW (1856–1950)

With life I am on the attack,
restlessly ferreting out
    each pleasure,
foraging for answers,
  wringing from it even the pain.
    I ransack life,
     hunt it down.

MARITA GOLDEN

*There are only two ways
to live your life.
One is as though nothing
is a miracle.
The other is as though
everything is a miracle.*

ALBERT EINSTEIN (1879–1955)

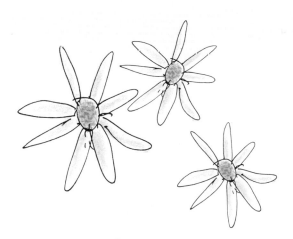

You should nurse your dreams
and protect them
through bad times
and tough times
to the sunshine
and light which always come.

WOODROW WILSON (1856–1924)

Keep on looking for the bright,
bright skies;
Keep on hoping that the sun will rise;
Keep on singing
when the whole world sighs,
And you'll get there in the morning.

SONG LYRICS

Like all people who have nothing,
I lived on dreams.

ANZIA YEZIERSKA, FROM "HUNGRY HEARTS"

*Our lives
are like the course of the sun.
At the darkest moment
there is the promise
of daylight.*

LONDON "TIMES" EDITORIAL,
DECEMBER 24, 1984

Hope ever urges on,
and tells us
tomorrow will be better.

TIBULLUS

Tomorrow is the most important
thing in life...
comes into us at midnight
very clean.
It's perfect when it arrives
and it puts itself
in our hands.

JOHN WAYNE (1907–1979)

Winter is on my head,
but eternal spring is in my heart.
The nearer I approach the end
the plainer I hear around me
the immortal symphonies
of the worlds which invite me.

VICTOR HUGO (1802–1885)

*In the depth of winter,
I finally learned that within me
there lay an invincible summer.*

ALBERT CAMUS (1913–1960)

*The future
belongs
to those who*
believe
*in the beauty
of their dreams.*

ELEANOR ROOSEVELT (1884–1962)

The world is round
and the place which may seem
like the end
may also be the beginning.

IVY BAKER PRIEST (1905–1975)

*The unendurable
is the beginning
of the curve of joy.*

DJUNA BARNES (1892–1982),
FROM "NIGHTWOOD"

Someone once said to me,
"Reverend Schuller,
I hope you live to see
all your dreams fulfilled."
I replied, "I hope not,
because if I live
and all my dreams are fulfilled,
I'm dead."
It's unfulfilled dreams
that keep you alive.

ROBERT SCHULLER, B.1926

Throw your heart
out in front of you
        And run ahead to catch it.

ARAB PROVERB

Even if I knew
        that the world
would end tomorrow,
        I would plant my apple tree today.

MARTIN LUTHER (1483–1546)

Do not linger
to gather flowers
to keep them,
but walk on,
for flowers
will keep themselves
blooming all your way.

RABINDRANATH TAGORE
(1861–1941)

LONGINGS INNUMERABLE
LONGINGS EXQUISITELY INTENSE!

HASHIM AMEER ALI

The longing for paradise
is paradise itself.

KAHLIL GIBRAN (1883–1931)

Hope
is the thing with feathers
That perches in the soul,
And sings the tune
without the words,
And never stops at all....

EMILY DICKINSON (1830–1886)

Helen Exley runs her own publishing company which sells giftbooks in more than seventy countries. She had always wanted to do a little book on smiles, and has been collecting the quotations for many years, but always felt that the available illustrations just weren't quite right. Then Helen fell in love with Joanna Kidney's happy, bright pictures and knew immediately they had the feel she was looking for. She asked Joanna to work on *smile*, and then to go on to contribute the art for four more books: *friend*, *happy day!*, *love* and *hope! dream!*

Joanna Kidney lives in County Wicklow in Ireland. She juggles her time between working on various illustration projects and producing her own art for shows and exhibitions. Her whole range of greeting cards *Joanna's Pearlies* – some of which appear in this book – won the prestigious 2001 Henries oscar for 'best fun or graphic range'.

Acknowledgements: The publishers are grateful for permission to reproduce copyright material. Whilst every reasonable effort has been made to trace copyright holders, the publishers would be pleased to hear from any not here acknowledged.
GEORGE BERNARD SHAW: From *Man and Superman* by George Bernard Shaw. Used with permission from The Society of Authors on behalf of the Bernard Shaw Estate.
PAM BROWN, CHARLOTTE GRAY: published with permission © Helen Exley 2003.